AUTHOR'S NOTE:This book was written by Gene Y. Michael in his private capacity. He is solely responsible for its content.

Gene Y. Michael received a bachelor of science degree in biology from Wake Forest University, a master of science degree in microbiology from Colorado State University, and a master of public administration degree from the University of Colorado. For 11 years, he worked for the city of Colorado Springs, serving first as the microbiologist and later as the environmental program administrator for the city's Department of Wastewater. His experience in the municipal wastewater industry includes working with state and federal agencies on discharge permit issues, water quality standards, and water quality regulations. Mr. Michael has designed and implemented water quality monitoring programs related both to wastewater treatment and to regional water quality management. To store and manage the large volumes of data generated by these monitoring programs, he established a computerized data management system. He served for 8 years on the regional water quality management committee, and is a member of the Water Pollution Control Federation, the American Water Resources Association, and the American Society for Microbiology. Mr. Michael is presently Vice President of Regulatory Management Inc. in Colorado Springs.

This book is dedicated to Ruth,
for her patience, support, and assistance.

Preface

This book outlines the process of computerizing a data base for the purpose of managing environmental data. It deals with the organizational philosophy that must underlie the successful implementation of a computerized environmental data base. The types of decisions that have to be made regarding objectives, data organization, software, hardware, and system management are described in general terms. The book is not intended to be a cookbook. Its purpose is to provide a conceptual framework that can aid the reader in thinking through the process of getting a successful computer system up and running.

Industries throughout the United States, including the municipal service industries, are becoming more aware of and interested in environmental protection. This interest mirrors the interest of the general public, as well as prudence stemming from the severe penalties associated with environmental laws. The volume of regulation requiring more environmental testing by many organizations is growing as well. Professional biologists, chemists, and engineers in environmental fields are increasingly faced with the problem of managing large volumes of data. They are being forced to establish computerized data bases, even though their training lies in other areas.

This book is not intended to provide a comprehensive treatment of computer data management topics, nor a technically detailed treatment of hardware and software capabilities. It is a broad outline of the issues that must be confronted in implementing a computerized environmental data base. This book does not deal with specific hardware or software products. The author is not an expert in computer systems and has not attempted to make an exhaustive survey of the hardware and software products available today.

In writing this book, the author assumed that the audience would comprise professionals in the environmental sciences who are computer literate but not computer professionals. It was supposed that readers would be generally familiar with different types of computer hardware and software and with data management concepts. Given this foundation, the book should provide more specific guidance in carrying out an environmental data base automation project.

Contents

3 Data Base Design

4 Software

5 Hardware

List of Figures

List of Tables

1

Introduction

1.1 EVOLUTION OF THE REGULATORY AGE

Concern for the environment has become a major force worldwide, and particularly in the United States. Environmental consciousness has spread to every level of present day American society. Citizens throughout the nation are bombarded daily with reports of leaks, spills, accidental releases, and discoveries of old chemical dumps leaching chemicals into soil, air, and water. In this climate where sensationalism sometimes outstrips common sense and new information shows that accepted waste disposal practices of yesterday are hazardous, the public understandably feels compelled to question all releases to the environment. Desires to eliminate dangerous and unesthetic pollution, to protect and improve our quality of life, and to preserve the environment for our descendants have been expressed by a series of national environmental protection laws. The growth of environmental concerns nationwide has spawned a burgeoning environmentalist lobby. At the federal level this lobby has encouraged ever more restrictive amendments to federal statutes, including expanded provisions encouraging citizen suits where it is perceived that regulatory agencies are not acting rapidly enough. This lobby has also engaged in several class action suits against EPA to force accelerated action in specific programs, or to force more stringent interpretation of specific statutes.

Each environmental statute engenders a series of regulations that specify the means of implementing the statute and, in effect, interpret the statute. The volume of regulation under different statutes has grown to the point where regulations overlap, placing multiple and sometimes conflicting requirements on dischargers. Perhaps a positive consequence of this regulatory bloat is that it is beginning to force a more holistic approach to environmental protection on regulators from different programs. Another consequence, which rises both from a more comprehensive world view of environmental protection and from burgeoning federal budgetary problems, is that a greater volume of general environmental data collection is being mandated than ever before, and dischargers are being required to provide it.

The U. S. Congress seems convinced that strict enforcement of environmental law is the most certain way to force more rapid progress toward the elimination of pollutant discharges. The liability accruing to violations of discharge permits has escalated from $10,000 to $25,000 per day of violation; prison terms for criminal convictions have doubled; bounties are provided to private citizens who bring charges against polluters. Sadly, annual EPA staff expansions go almost exclusively to attorneys for enforcement programs, while scientific staff additions for technical assistance and research are almost nil. Moreover, to satisfy congressional pressures for quick, visible coups, efforts focus mainly on the easy targets—point source dischargers with existing permits—rather than taking on more difficult issues such as nonpoint sources.

1.2 USES OF ENVIRONMENTAL DATA BASES

Industries in both the private and public sectors that discharge treated waste streams to natural systems now find themselves in a very awkward position. On the one hand, they operate in a society dominated by consumer demand which drives a free market economy. On the other hand, no matter how high the consumer demand for a product whose manufacture creates a pollutant waste stream, and no matter how necessary a service a public utility may serve, the public is increasingly intolerant of even those pollutant discharges that comply with regulations and permit conditions.

Environmental monitoring programs and data bases are positive, proactive approaches that organizations can use to demonstrate commitment to environmental protection, to devise business plans which protect environmental quality, to establish better community relations and foster a productive relationship with the public, and, in the extreme, to defend themselves against inappropriate charges of harming the environment. Solid environmental monitoring programs must be comprehensive and farsighted. They are not simple or inexpensive. However, the cost of maintaining a sound environmental monitoring program is lower than the cost of being unable to show that waste treatment operations are effective and that a good faith effort has been made to protect the environment. Those costs are measured in terms of the costs of litigation, fines, construction of advanced waste treatment facilities, damaged reputations, and the loss of community trust.

Environmental data bases serve a variety of purposes. These are summarized in Table 1.

1.2.A Documentation of Existing Conditions

Environmental data bases document existing environmental conditions as a basis for regulatory and management decisions. Environmental statutes are generally administered through permitting programs. A discharge permit controls the activities of individual permittees. A discharge permit is a contractual document that establishes legally binding conditions, including limits on the quality of emissions to the environment. These limits are derived from calculations

Table 1   Functions Supported by Environmental Data Bases

- Baseline documentation
- Modeling
- Identify seasonal and diurnal patterns
- Identify spatial and temporal trends
- Correlate end-of-process quality with environmental quality
- Avoid or support litigation

based on environmental standards or existing environmental conditions. Discharge limits assure that environmental standards are not violated as a result of the emission. Permit writers seldom have the resources to obtain comprehensive data about existing conditions. Instead they proceed on the basis of existing data whether it be old, incomplete, or patently inaccurate. The burden is on the permittee to develop an accurate data base to support permitting decisions.

1.2.B Modeling

Mathematical models are useful tools both in the permitting process and in providing a rational basis for facility and area-wide planning. To provide reliable results, however, models must be calibrated using data that accurately describe existing conditions. Following calibration, and periodically throughout their useful life, models must be verified by demonstrating that they accurately predict existing conditions based on background data. The environmental data bases become the source of calibration and verification data.

1.2.C Characterization of Cycles

Natural systems are characterized by regular seasonal and daily variations. These natural cycles have great implications for permit writing because they define critical or limiting conditions under which the impact of emissions on the environment are maximized. Like all natural phenomena, these cycles vary in their timing and intensity in different locations. Like all permitting issues, there is rarely complete information on hand to describe these cycles, so permit writers proceed on the basis of general assumptions that may be completely inappropriate. Environmental data bases characterize seasonal and diurnal cycles, providing solid information upon which to base rational permitting decisions.

1.2.D Spatial and Temporal Trends

The identification of the sources of environmental impacts is the first step in their solution. Spatial and temporal trends in environmental quality, documented by environmental data bases, help to identify impacts and to point to their sources. The success of environmental control programs is documented by temporal trends in environmental quality. A discharger can use a demonstration of improving temporal trends very effectively in demonstrating compliance with regulations and statutes. From a defensive standpoint, environmental data bases can help to distinguish the environmental impacts caused by a specific discharger from impacts arising from other sources.

1.2.E Correlation of End-of-Process Quality with Environmental Quality

Environmental data bases can help to influence regulatory decisions and policies at both the state and federal levels. Environmental standards are usually based on an assumption that the results of laboratory tests are representative of effects in natural systems. Despite the fact that laboratory test systems are far simpler than the natural environment, it is assumed that there is a direct and simple relationship between the content of an emission and the quality of the local environment. Fortunately for mankind, such assumptions are almost never true. Unfortunately, researchers developing environmental standards seldom have the resources to conduct the exhaustive field analyses required to collect truly representative data. A good environmental data base can demonstrate the adequacy of environmental standards and provide grounds for revision. Environmental data bases can also help to correlate the quality of emissions to environmental quality, providing a basis for the development of site-specific permit conditions which are allowed under all regulatory programs.

1.2.F Litigation Avoidance and Support

In the final extremity, environmental data bases can help to avoid or support litigation. Portions of environmental statutes have been written broadly, with the intent that regulatory agencies (federal or state) will fill in the necessary detail through regulation. Unfortunately, regulations are not always completely clear, and disputes sometimes arise as to whether the requirements of statute and regulation have been satisfied. When such disputes go beyond the specific procedural requirements of permits, environmental data bases may be the only source of information which can demonstrate whether the environment has been protected by existing operating procedures. Where adequate data exist in advance of a dispute, presentation of such data can help permittees convince regulatory authorities that no basis for enforcement actions exists. Where an enforcement action has been undertaken, timely development of an appropriate environmental data base may supply critical evidence showing the lack of environmental harm, and providing a basis for avoiding or mitigating penalties. Naturally, it is incumbent upon the discharger to be aware of any environmental harm his discharge may cause and to take immediate and effective action to eliminate such harm. No environmental data base can or should protect a discharger who does not pursue a responsible course of action.

1.3 ENVIRONMENTAL MONITORING PROGRAMS

Environmental data bases are the repositories for data generated by environmental monitoring programs. The value of the environmental data base is directly dependent on the care with which the monitoring program is designed and implemented.

1.3.A Goals and Objectives

Both environmental monitoring programs and environmental data bases should be based on carefully thought out goals and objectives. Short-term goals might be the collection of data required to support the next permit renewal, or data collection designed to evaluate the impact of a pending regulatory program. Long-term goals might focus on environmental quality trends over time and beyond the immediate vicinity of the discharge, on collection of data to use in the calibration and verification of models, or on the identification of sources of known impacts.

Setting appropriate goals for environmental data bases is no easy task. An organization must focus on the present, assessing current conditions constantly and remaining alert for any environmental impacts its discharges may have. It must look to the future, assessing the possibility that non-compliance with environmental regulations could result from growth, from expansion into new areas of activity, or from revised or entirely new environmental regulations. But it must also track the past, for only by comparing where the organization is to where the organization has been can it be determined whether current efforts are driving the organization in the right direction.

1.3.B Philosophy, Maintenance, and Funding

The types of support that organizations must provide to maintain effective environmental monitoring and data man-

Table 2   Organizational Support for Environmental Data Bases

- Organizational policy must support data collection and management
- Funding must be adequate
- Rationale and goals must be documented to maintain continuity

agement programs are summarized in Table 2. In planning an environmental monitoring program, it is a disastrous mistake to take too narrow an approach, assuming that the organization should be responsible for monitoring only in its immediate vicinity. Parochialism is an easy trap to fall into because resources are always short. It is the nature of fiscal management, in both the public and private sectors, never to give any program all the support requested. With respect to environmental data bases, however, it must always be recalled that as a discharger you affect others at a distance, even as others affect you. The purpose of environmental monitoring programs and their environmental data bases is to detect, define, and document these effects. Therefore, neither geographic coverage nor the scope of parameters tested should be limited too severely, or the program will likely fail to fulfill its purpose.

Maintenance of environmental data bases is expensive, requiring trained sampling personnel, highly qualified analysts operating expensive equipment, and experts to interpret data and produce useful information. The high costs of monitoring make budget directors cringe and lead to continual calls to reduce monitoring. There is false economy in heeding these calls. Compare the cost of a $100,000 annual monitoring program to a two-week period of violating an environmental standard, at a civil penalty assessment of $10,000 per day—or at a criminal penalty assessment of $25,000 per day. If the budget director were to assume responsibility for these costs, then he would have a right to call for monitoring program reductions. However, a CEO who can be held personally liable for environmental damage or permit violations is well advised to keep his monitoring program funded!

Another frustration is the feeling that environmental monitoring is done just for the sake of doing studies. Most of the time, environmental monitoring produces no visible result, and it never ends. Environmental monitoring is analogous to paying large fire insurance premiums for years without a fire. You have to keep reminding yourself and others that, as in the case of fire insurance, when the day comes that you need environmental monitoring data, you will need it badly; not having the data will mean ruin. The rapid rate of change in the regulatory arena is a major difficulty. A major scientific finding can occur at any time showing that an accepted practice is actually damaging to the environment. Worse, a sudden shift in public opinion may focus attention overnight on an area which has never previously been considered. An example from the water quality field is the chlorination of treated wastewater for disinfection, to prevent the spread of waterborne diseases. As recently as 1910, yellow fever accounted for a high percentage of the mortalities in persons below the age of 50 in the United States. The disinfection of treated wastewater with chlorine has virtually eliminated yellow fever. However, due to the more recent recognition that residual chlorine is harmful to aquatic organisms, the EPA is now encouraging the elimination of chlorination except in specific cases, even though no equally effective disinfection technologies are available.

There are only two unvarying rules in environmental management. First, when you need data, you need it instantly. Second, by the time you find out what data you really need, it is too late for data collection. The only defense is to maintain an environmental monitoring program that is broader than you need most of the time, in order to be sure that the emergencies are covered.

Discontinuities in the data base are deadly to trend analysis and thus to negotiating posture. Although regulatory agencies are willing to write permits with next to no data of their own, they demand perfection when a discharger's data base is used. Modelers and statisticians are stymied by gaps in historical data and are forced to rely on estimates and assumptions that are so highly qualified as to damage the credibility of the findings.

Effective environmental monitoring programs and environmental data bases require secure organizational support. This support must include at least three basic elements. First, organizational policy must clearly support the goals and objectives of environmental monitoring and environmental data base maintenance. Second, adequate funding must be committed to assure that the environmental monitoring program is adequate to meet the needs of the organization. Third, sufficient documentation must be developed to establish the rationale behind environmental monitoring and to establish the long term monitoring goals, in order that the continuity of the monitoring effort is protected.

1.3.C Types of Environmental Monitoring Programs

Ongoing environmental monitoring programs are designed to characterize environmental quality over time and over a broad geographical area. Sampling stations may be quite far apart, providing little information about specific local conditions. Because of the long-term nature of such monitoring programs, sampling is seldom more frequent than monthly and often is as infrequent as quarterly or semi-annually. Ongoing monitoring programs often involve a large number of parameters.

Synoptic environmental monitoring programs are designed either to gather a great deal of information within a short period of time over a restricted geographical area or to characterize time-dependent natural cycles within a short period of time. Synoptic programs often involve a large number of sampling stations located close together so that spatial variations in environmental conditions are illuminated. Synoptic programs aimed at measuring diurnal cycles may involve hourly sampling at each monitoring station throughout a 24-hour period. Synoptic programs may be used to collect calibration and verification data for modeling efforts.

Issue-specific environmental monitoring programs are designed to address specific questions, and their design is as varied as the range of potential questions. They often deal with identifying specific sources of pollutants or causes of adverse effects, and they end when the sources are identified.

2

Data Requirements

2.1 DATA BASE TERMINOLOGY

Environmental data bases need not be more complex than a family checkbook. However, as is the case in every branch of science and technology, environmental data bases are described using a jargon that can be confusing.

Think of a data base as a table written on a sheet of paper, similar to a checkbook register. In a checkbook register, each line documents pertinent information about a single transaction. For each check there is a record of the check number, the date it was written, the amount paid, and the person or business to whom payment was made. A running balance is usually the final column. Other columns may provide space to record whether a check has been reconciled with the bank statement, any fee associated with the check, or an additional memorandum about the purpose of the expenditure. The computer software used to manage the data base is called a **data base management system (DBMS)**.

In data base terminology, each line from the check register is a **record**. A record contains all the elements needed to describe completely a unique piece of data. Each column from the check register is a **field**. Fields organize records so that the elements of each record fall into the same order, making it easy to compare records and summarize the data they represent. The **structural design** of the data base deals with the fields included in each record and with the order of fields within the records. In data base terminology, the entire check register might be called a **table**, a **file**, or a **data base**.

Often several checks are entered into the check register on a given day. This results in checks being entered in order by check number and by date. An exception could occur if a post-dated check were written, as when a check is written on Saturday morning to pay a bill due the following Wednesday and given Wednesday's date. If more checks are written later on Saturday and given Saturday's date, then the check register might be in order by check number but out of order by date. If it later becomes necessary to summarize payments by date, reordering the records would be required. In data base terminology this is called **sorting** or **ordering**. It might be necessary to examine only those checks paid to a particular vendor or all checks written during a particular week. In data base terminology these are examples of **selective retrievals**, where only those records fitting defined criteria are considered. Retrieving data from electronic data bases is done by means of **query statements**, which specify the criteria that describe the data to be retrieved. Most data base software uses some type of **query language**, which consists of a set of key works that the software recognizes as standard descriptors for elements of data records and for actions to be performed. One such query language is called structured query language or **SQL** (pronounced "sequel" as an acronym), which is used by several mainframe data base programs.

Data base software consists of complex programs whose main function is to organize, store, and retrieve data. Trade-offs may be made with respect to the sophistication of mathematical and statistical functions and graphics functions built into the data base. Separate software specializing in these functions can be used to enhance the utility of environmental data. Such specialized software is referred to in this book as **companion software**. Companion software is discussed in Section 4.4.

Table 1   Uses for Environmental Data

- Summary reports
- Regulatory reports
- Real-time operations control
- Research
- Litigation

There are three generally recognized types of computer-ized data bases. These are **hierarchical, networking,** and **relational** data bases. Relational data bases represent the current state of the art. A major advantage of relational data bases is that two or more data bases or tables can be easily combined. In a business setting, a company will have sepa-rate data bases for its accounting and personnel functions. However, there will be instances in which operations in one area need data from the other, as when the accounting department needs the hourly wages of employees to project overhead expenses. In an environmental setting, a munici-pal wastewater treatment plant may have separate data bases summarizing effluent quality and receiving stream quality. In order to determine whether a correlation between effluent quality and in-stream quality exists, it is necessary to combine data from the two data bases. Relational data bases are designed to accommodate these needs and are able to accomplish such tasks easily.

2.2 UTILIZATION OF DATA

The design of environmental data bases is based on the uses that will be made of the data in the data base. Common uses for environmental data are summarized in Table 1. Design of the environmental data bases should make the most frequent or the most important applications easiest, while accommodating all other potential applications. Some applications that an environmental data base should support are discussed below.

2.2.A Summary Reports

Summary reports are the simplest uses of environmental data bases. They display monitoring results at specified locations during specified time periods for specified parameters. Summary statistics such as averages, maxima, and minima may be included. Graphical presentation of data may also be included. Summary reports provide a cursory look at data for those who need a rapid scan of existing conditions or the status of the monitoring program, rather than in-depth analyses of trends or interpretations of the data.

2.2.B Regulatory Reports

All discharges regulated through permits require reporting to regulatory authorities. Regulatory reports require certifications as to their completeness and correctness from the responsible officers of the organization. Thus, for the protection of corporate officers, the contents of regulatory reports must be protected from errors through quality control procedures. These procedures include review of data before it is entered into the data base as well as review of the data base to assure completeness and accuracy. They may also include automatic checks, such as screening values as they are entered to assure that the entries fall within historical ranges or identifying duplicate records. Additionally, the requirements of regulatory reports establish the minimum requirements for fields within the data base. Changes in regulatory reporting requirements will likely require the addition of new fields, so the data base software should be carefully screened to ensure that it accommodates the easy addition of fields.

2.2.C Real-Time Operations Control

A few discharge permits are written with limits that vary with environmental conditions. An example is a water quality discharge permit in which permit limits vary with the current flow levels of the receiving stream. Permit limits that vary seasonally are not uncommon, being based on seasonal climatic patterns or on seasonal patterns of natural resource uses. Where such permits exist, facility operators may require very current environmental data to manage waste treatment processes.

2.2.D Research

There is infinite variety in nature and an infinite variety of ways to achieve a desired level of environmental protection. It is the goal of all who discharge waste streams to achieve the appropriate level of environmental protection at the lowest possible cost and with the greatest degree of simplicity. Achievement of this goal is enhanced by a thorough understanding of the natural systems that waste streams may impact. From a practical standpoint, discharge permitting programs have come to rely on standardized requirements and approaches. Regulations allow modifications of standard requirements, if the desired modifications are technically supportable. The burden of demonstrating technical feasibility rests with the applicant. Environmental data bases are an important tool that can be used to the advantage of an applicant in demonstrating the technical feasibility of a modified permitting method.

2.2.E Litigation

Litigation may be threatened against a discharger for alleged violations of permit limits or for allegedly causing environmental degradation. Where such actions result from negligence or criminal conduct, there can be little question that the most severe penalties allowed by statute are justified. Unfortunately, there can be many other sources for such actions. These may include operational failures of waste treatment processes for a host of reasons beyond the control of the discharger. Where permit language is unclear, allowing for different interpretations of permit limits or other

Table 2   Data Elements

Required Data	Chain of Custody Data	Desirable Data

• Sample date
• Sample time
• Sample source
• Identity of sampler
	• Sample collection method
	• Sample preservation
	• Sample identification
	• Persons in custody of and security of sample during:
	  ► transportation
	  ► analysis
	  ► storage
	• Review of analysis
		• Identity of analyst
		• Analysis data
		• Analytical method
		• Date of entry into data base

conditions, disputes over compliance status can arise. Vague provisions of environmental statutes or regulations for which a regulatory agency's interpretation may change over time can cause disputes over compliance status. Environmentalist groups or private citizens who disagree with the provisions of environmental statutes or regulations may file class action suits under the citizen suit provisions of environmental statutes. In all these cases, environmental data bases serve as essential elements of defense. They demonstrate whether actual environmental degradation occurred or is likely to have occurred, they establish limits on the real amount of harm that may have occurred, and they provide a rational basis for quantifying risk. Environmental data bases can provide pivotal evidence that relieves a discharger of unwarranted liability or provides evidence that justifies mitigation of penalties.

2.3 DATA

Environmental data elements may be divided into three types: minimum data elements required to establish a usable context for a measurement, chain of custody data, and desirable data. These data types are summarized in Table 2.

2.3.A Minimum Data Elements

There are eight data elements that should be associated with all environmental measurements. These elements are often specified as requirements directly in discharge permits. The minimum data elements are

1. date of sample collection
2. time of sample collection
3. location of sample collection
4. identity of the sampler
5. parameter for which analysis was performed
6. analytical result
7. units in which the analytical result is expressed
8. remarks (i. e., indeterminate data symbols)

Beyond the fact that these are the minimum data elements required to establish a usable context for an analytical result, these data elements make it possible to aggregate and select specified types of data in meaningful ways. With these data elements it becomes possible to examine spatial trends comparing the values of a parameter at different stations or to examine temporal trends by comparing the values of a parameter at a given station at different times. It even becomes possible to examine the efficiency of samplers by comparing the analytical results from their samples.

2.3.B Chain of Custody Data

Chain of custody data consist of detailed records of sample handling. Such records document how and by whom a sample was collected, preserved, identified, transported, stored, and analyzed. They show how analytical results are reported, reviewed, and verified. The purpose of chain of custody records is to show that a given analytical result is reasonably expected to be valid, for purposes of law. To make this demonstration it is necessary to document carefully all steps from the point of sampling to the point of reporting the final analytical result. Of particular importance is the recording of personal custody of the sample at all times, to show whether an opportunity occurred for some party to tamper with the sample or to substitute another sample in order to alter the analytical result, or whether samples could have been misidentified. Solid chain of custody data are essential where analytical results are used in litigation. Although maintaining chain of custody records is tedious and time consuming, keeping such records should be made standard practice. If continuous records are not maintained, they cannot be reconstructed after the fact, and it is seldom possible to anticipate when they will be needed.

2.3.C Desirable Data

Certain data are simply nice to have. They provide the opportunity to perform a whole series of checks on analytical results in the event that questions arise or anomalies in the data occur. Where possible, it is strongly advisable to maintain these data as part of the principal data base. Although these data can be archived in the form of laboratory bench sheets or analyst notebooks, this practice makes retrieval difficult, cumbersome, and time consuming. The result is that retrieval and examination of such data is rarely performed, and simple explanations for apparent anomalies remain undiscovered. This can cast doubt on the validity of the data base.

2.3.C.1 Analyst

The name of the analyst can be important for verifying data which do not appear to fit normal patterns, or in the event that a significant change in average values for a parameter coincides with a change in analysts.

2.3.C.2 Analysis Date

As analysts change, so do analytical instruments, calibration standards, sample preparation technicians, and sources of laboratory chemical supplies. Records of analysis dates can help identify such occurrences and relate them to anomalous data.

2.3.C.3 Analytical Method

Chemical analyses can be performed by a variety of methods. Each method is sensitive to different sources of interference and has a different detection limit. Such information may be important to chain of custody records and may help to explain different results obtained on split samples, where a sample is subdivided and analyzed by different laboratories to check the accuracy of results. Additionally, certain methods are formally approved by regulatory agencies, while other equivalent methods are not, simply because of the level of effort and expense involved for the regulatory agency to certify all available methods. Again, such information may be important to litigation.

2.3.C.4 Detection Limit

Each chemical analysis procedure has a detection limit, below or near which the accuracy of the analytical result becomes suspect. The detection limit literally changes each time the procedure is run and should be calculated for each run. It is very important to know the detection limit associated with a result, in order to gauge the reliability of the result. Additionally, chemical analyses of environmental samples frequently do not detect the parameter being analyzed. This result is commonly reported as being less than the detection limit. It is important to know what the detection limit was. Was the detection limit reasonable with respect to an environmental standard? If a water quality standard for a metal is set at 20 mg/L and the detection limit of the test procedure is 50 mg/L, no useful information is provided by a "less-than-detection-limit" result because it is not possible to determine whether compliance was attained. There are statistical techniques available to estimate values for results that fall below detection limits, but it is completely inappropriate to use the detection limit itself for the computation of statistics other than maximum and minimum probability bounds. Thus, it is necessary to know detection limits associated with analytical results and to flag results reported as below detection limits clearly in the data base so they are not used inappropriately.

2.3.C.5 *Date of Data Entry into the Data Base*

Another source of incorrect data in an electronic data base is the transcription of data from paper to computer. Operator error is perhaps the most common cause, but errors and data base corruption can also result from power surges, bad disk or tape sectors, transmission line noise between remote sites, difficulties in restoring data from backup storage during recovery from a computer crash, and the myriad unidentified things that go wrong with computers which computer professionals collectively refer to as "glitches." Data base corruption can result from changes in the data base structure, which is almost inevitable at some point. Knowledge of the date of data entry allows correlation with such events or with specific data entry personnel.

3

Data Base Design

3.1 ESTABLISHING GOALS AND OBJECTIVES

Knowing what questions you want to answer is as funda-mental to the process of data base design as it is to the process of monitoring program design. The idea is to deter-mine who needs the data and how they will use it, then design the data base so that it will support all foreseeable applications and do the most important ones easily. This process can be difficult. Applications change rapidly in response to changing regulations, and users find it difficult to make comprehensive lists even of their existing applica-tions. An outline for the process is provided in Table 1.

Determining the applications that the data base will be required to support requires significant organizational effort. One means of beginning to develop a list of applications is to prompt users by listing the data that is presently available as well as the data new monitoring programs are designed to collect. This gives users a sense of the scope of the data base. Listing current uses of data, such as process monitoring and completion of regulatory reports, may bring other possible uses to mind. Soliciting information about upcoming pro-jects such as permit renewals, organizational expansions, or pending environmental issues may identify new data uses or

Table 1   Determining Environmental Data Base Applications

- List existing data
- List new data needs
- List existing and future uses of data
- Examine planned projects
- Use questionnaires, interviews, group meetings
- Involve personnel at all levels of the organization including operations, laboratory, clerical, and management
- Provide feedback via interim reports

new data needs. Canvassing the organization for data base applications should not be confined to management. Be sure to talk to the field collection personnel and laboratory technicians to gain an appreciation for the level of detail available. Talk to the data entry personnel to identify factors that make data entry easier, thus reducing transcription error. Talk to clerical personnel to get details on the information required for reports.

A variety of techniques including questionnaires, interviews, and meetings should be used to gather the requisite information. Questionnaires provide a vehicle for summarizing existing data availability and uses and provide respondents an opportunity to mull their answers. Interviews provide for interaction between the user and the data base designer, which the data base designer can use to draw out additional information about the operation of the organization and gain a better understanding of data uses. Meetings provide an opportunity for users to cross-fertilize ideas and applications as well as enhance understanding by all participants of how the sections of the organization interact. Interim reports should be provided, apprising users of the information the data base designer has received and the conclusions drawn by the designer regarding data base structure. It frequently proves easier for users to flesh out a skeleton proposal than to design the data base from scratch, and interim reports can provide a skeleton.

Table 2   Considerations in Environmental Data Base Automation

- Ease of data entry and retrieval
- Speed
- Manipulation power
  - ►Complexity of selective retrievals
  - ►Multiple level sorts and data grouping
  - ►Joining records
  - ►Mathematical and statistical functions
  - ►Graphics
  - ►Report formatting
- Data storage format

3.2 AUTOMATION

Computer systems consist of both machinery (**hardware**) and programs (**software**). Basic considerations involving automation of a data base include the ease of data entry and retrieval, speed, power for manipulation, companion software, and quality requirements for output. These considerations, summarized in Table 2, relate both to software and hardware.

3.2.A Ease of Data Entry and Retrieval

The value of an electronic data base lies in giving users the ability to enter data easily at random as it becomes available, and later to retrieve only those data currently of interest, in a specified order which makes examination of the data easy. There is a wide spectrum of data base software available, representing programs of greater or lesser degrees of power and user-friendliness. Although it seems, intuitively, that a more powerful program would be more difficult to use, such is not necessarily the case. The ease of use depends on the care the programmer took in preparing the user interface — the prompts, command syntax requirements, screen displays, on-line help modules, manuals, and tutorials that train the user and guide the user through various procedures. Software that is difficult to use can intimidate casual users, frustrate power users, and generally become more trouble to use than it is worth. This destroys the value of the data base. Well-engineered software encourages casual users to examine and analyze data, makes in-depth data analysis and detailed report preparation easy for power users, and maximizes the value of the data base.

Easy data entry is important to minimize transcription errors and to encourage data entry personnel to keep data entry up to date. Color monitors ease data entry by high-lighting entry fields, reducing eye strain, and helping to focus the attention of the operator. On-screen graphics and prompts highlight entry fields, focus attention, and explain input fields. Some data base software packages provide on-line help facilities to explain the usage of input fields in depth. Many data base software packages offer automatic range screening on numeric entry fields. Automatic range screening checks entries into selected fields and either pre-vents entry of numbers that fall outside the specified range or at least provides a signal that the data entry operator must override manually if an out-of-range entry is in fact correct. Automatic screening helps to eliminate simple transcription errors such as reversed digits and misplaced decimals.

Easy data retrieval maximizes the value of the data base by encouraging users to examine and analyze data. Casual users may prefer menu-driven data query systems because of their simplicity. Menu-driven query systems typically list the available fields and prompt the user to specify the fields of interest, the parameters for limiting searches, and the order in which data should be displayed. More advanced users may find menu-driven query systems cumbersome and slow. Advanced users may prefer an English-like query system, which uses a structured syntax form to allow users to enter sequences of commands specifying the conditions for data retrievals in the form of abbreviated sentences. A few data base software packages provide both menu-driven and structured query language formats.

3.2.B Speed

The speed with which a computerized data base enters and retrieves data depends on both hardware and software factors. Hardware factors include the system architecture, the configuration and characteristics of disks and monitors, and the number of simultaneous users on the system. Software factors include the size of the data base and the techniques used by the program to index, search, and sort data.

Speed becomes a more important consideration as the size of the data base increases. A user may find it acceptable to wait 15 to 20 seconds for a selective retrieval and sort operation. However, a 15 second operation on a data base of 500 records becomes something much longer on a data base of 100,000 records, and one function of environmental data bases is to grow. An approach that might be useful in designing an environmental data base is to examine the size of the existing data base and to project its growth over five years, and design the system to accommodate the five-year planning horizon. Computer technology changes so rapidly that when system modifications become necessary after five years, hardware and companion software options are likely to be much improved, and quite possibly less expensive as well.

3.2.C Power for Manipulation

Power for manipulation refers to the ability of the data base software to perform a wide variety of tasks such as complex selective retrievals, multiple level sorts, data grouping, joining data bases or retrieving data from several data bases simultaneously, formatting reports, performing mathematical and statistical calculations, displaying the results of mathematical and statistical calculations graphically, and creating data files for use by companion software.

3.2.C.1 Complexity of Selective Retrievals

Selective data retrievals from environmental data bases are most often based on a parameter and location. However, it may be desirable to limit a retrieval to a period between specific dates to investigate a specific incident. It may be desirable to limit a retrieval to the summer or winter months to investigate seasonal variations, or to limit a retrieval to specific times of day to investigate diurnal cycles. It may be necessary to combine several of these limitations or to retrieve data where either one set of complex criteria are satisfied or another set of criteria are satisfied. It may be easiest to make a retrieval exclusionary rather than inclusive; that is, to retrieve data records which do not satisfy a set of criteria. The query language used by the data base software should provide a complete range of options for complex retrievals.

3.2.C.2 Multiple Level Sorts and Data Grouping

Grouping data into categories provides a logical organization which makes it easier to comprehend. For summary reports, it may be desirable to organize data from an environmental monitoring network by sampling station, by date from earliest to latest within each station, by hour from earliest to latest for each date, and finally by parameter. For regression analyses, it may be desirable to combine the results of two or more parameters from each station into columns of matched data sets and sort the columns according to the parameter selected as the independent variable, in ascending order. Different retrievals will require limiting the fields displayed for each record and changing the order of the fields according to the purpose at hand. The data base software should be capable of providing a wide range of options and capabilities with regard to organizing data retrievals.

3.2.C.3 Joining Records

Data bases generally treat records as independent, unique sets. However, it may sometimes be desirable to combine pieces from different records into a single record for purposes of computation. For example, if the decision is made during data base design to structure records so that each record represents only the result of a single parameter analysis (see Section 3.2.D below), the computations requiring the use of several pieces of data may require that those data be merged into a single record. Some data bases deal with this problem poorly if at all, requiring the construction of temporary files and multiple-step matching procedures. Other data bases have report writing modules that can perform both the functions of combining records and calculation. A third way to accomplish the task of combining records is to have companion software perform the joining process.

3.2.C.4 Joining Data Bases

Often the need arises to use data from different data bases in reports or analytical procedures. For example, separate data bases may be maintained for data collected by environmental monitoring programs and for data related to an industrial process. The process of renewing a discharge permit will require that environmental impacts be projected by comparing waste stream data to environmental standards. The permit application process is streamlined by the ability to pull data from the two separate data bases into a single file for calculation and reporting. Relational data bases perform this task with ease; this is the task for which they were developed. Other forms of electronic data storage may make the process difficult.

3.2.C.5 Mathematical and Statistical Functions

Many relational data bases were developed for business applications. While these data bases may offer excellent features for storing and retrieving data and for report writing, they may offer only basic mathematical functions and summary statistics used commonly in business. Thus the built-in math functions are often unsuitable for scientific applications, such as any calculation that requires exponentiation. Some data base software, designed for technical applications, provide high-powered mathematical capabilities. However, they often trade off some other sophisticated capabilities such as easy redesign of the data base.

The lack of advanced mathematical functions as an integral part of data base software may not be a severe limitation. As a practical matter, arithmetic averages and standard deviations often represent the useful limit of sophistication. Quality control curves can be generated using these functions. The wide range of mathematical functions and statistical tests that have been developed for various purposes makes it a practical impossibility for data base software to incorporate a wide enough range to satisfy the needs of more than a few groups of users. The availability of companion software, such as electronic spreadsheets, reduces the importance of the general lack of advanced mathematical functions.

3.2.C.6 Graphics

Graphs represent an effective, and hence an important, means of summarizing data and presenting the results of analyses. Many generic data base programs provide relatively limited graphics capabilities. Their capabilities are limited relative to the wide range of sophisticated graphics software packages that are tailored to specific applications in business and science. As is the case with mathematical functions, the easy availability of companion graphics software reduces the importance of this limitation.

3.2.C.7 Report Formatting

It is often said about our modern society that perception is reality; that it is not enough to be right in order to win, you must also look good. The importance of the ability to produce reports that are clear, easy to read, easy to understand, and pleasant to the eye cannot be overstated. Moreover, it is essential that report preparation be as easy as possible. Reports are the means by which raw data and the results of analyses are transmitted to management, to regulators, and to an often skeptical public. Poorly designed reports that are unclear, confusing, and fail to focus the attention of the reader on significant information result in inappropriate management policies, improper regulation, and poor public relations.

Data base programs often use **report writers**, which may either be integrated into the data base software or sold as an add-on module, to make report formatting easier. Basic report writing capabilities include formatting numeric columns, assigning column headings, changing the order of columns, providing summary statistics, and establishing page width and length. These are functions of the data base software itself, associated with the data retrieval process. More sophisticated capabilities such as combining graphics and text, multicolumn text, and multiple fonts can be provided by companion software and hardware. These options are discussed in greater detail in Section 4.4.

3.2.D Data Storage Format

Planning the data storage format consists of deciding what data is to be captured and how fields are to be organized within records. Remember to think of a data base as a two-dimensional matrix, where rows are records and columns are fields. Fields contain types of information about data points, such as dates, locations, and values. Each record must contain all the fields required to describe a single point of data completely, but may contain more fields. The design of the data storage format depends on the most common uses for data and on the capabilities of the data base software. The basic considerations related to selecting a data storage format are summarized in Table 3.

Table 3   Data Storage Format Considerations

- Flexibility
- Ease of computation
- Indeterminate data

The data storage format can either enhance flexibility for selective data retrievals or enhance ease of computation. The data storage format can be designed to either treat individual data points as unique records or to treat more complex data assemblages as unique records. A record format that incorporates all the analytical result fields and all the qualifier fields for each parameter measured at a sampling location on a given day is an example of a more complex data assemblage. This record format treats the combination of monitoring station and date as the unique record identifier. Another example is a record format that incorporates all the sampling times, all analytical results, and all qualifiers for samples collected on a given day from all monitoring stations. This record format treats the sampling date as the unique record identifier.

Where individual data points are treated as unique records, only fields that include the minimal essential elements to describe an individual data point are part of the record: sampling location, date, time, parameter, value, units, and a qualifier field (Figure 1). The parameter field contains a code that identifies the physical or chemical parameter measured. The value field contains the analytical result. The qualifier field may be used to flag analytical results that were below detection limits.

Where records represent more complex data assemblages, the data storage format may become quite complex. Each parameter result and qualifier may be assigned a separate field. If the monitoring program includes a large number of monitoring stations, a large number of parameters, or involves sampling more than once per day, the length of the record required to accommodate this format may make the use of such a complex record configuration impractical. Further, whenever monitoring stations or

LOCATION	DATE	TIME	PARAMETER CODE	VALUE	QUALIFIER	SAMPLER

Figure 1 The minimal record format provides maximum flexibility and ease of adding parameters. Computations requiring the use of parameters contained in different records may be complicated.

parameters are added to the monitoring program, the structure of the data base has to be revised.

3.2.D.1 Maximum Flexibility

A minimal record format simplifies the formulation of complex retrieval statements and increases the speed with which the data records can be searched. Depending on the capabilities of the data base software, a minimal record configuration may make it possible to specify a greater number of limiting factors for data retrievals than would be possible if the record configuration were more complex.

Another major advantage of the minimal record configuration is the ease of adding new parameters. In the minimal configuration, a field must be provided to contain a code identifying sampling location or the physical or chemical parameter that the analytical result represents. Adding a new sampling location or parameter is a simple matter of developing a new location or parameter code. No modifications of the data base structure are required. On the other hand, if a complex record configuration is designed to be unique to a sampling station and date, then separate fields would represent values for different parameters. To add a parameter, it would be necessary to change the structure of the data base. Depending on the capabilities of the data base, this procedure is time consuming at least. It may be cumbersome and even dangerous. Changing data base structure destroys the data in the current data base. It is usually necessary to copy the data base into a new file, modify the data base structure, and then update the new data base from the old data files. If this procedure has to be performed manually, requiring an operator to name, open, copy, and close temporary files, there is a greater danger of permanent data loss.

A disadvantage of the minimal record configuration is that it may prove difficult to combine values from different records for purposes of computation. For example, in the water quality field, the concentration of un-ionized ammonia is of interest from the standpoint of protecting fish. Un-ionized ammonia concentrations must be calculated using the temperature, pH, and total ammonia concentration at the time of sampling. With a minimal record configuration, these data are contained in separate records. Depending on the capabilities of the data base software, using data from separate records for computation may be cumbersome or impossible. It may be necessary to use a report writer or companion software to accomplish the task.

3.2.D.2 Ease of Computation

The advantage of using a data storage format that treats more complex data assemblages as unique records (Figure 2) is that complex record formats enhance the ease of computation by placing all data collected during a single sampling event in a single record. Most data base programs deal easily with mathematical operations that involve fields within a given record, so complex record formats maximize the ease of computations.

Complex record formats have several disadvantages. First, it is more difficult to add new parameters, as described in previous sections. Second, complex record structure results in large, cumbersome tables. It may prove more difficult to perform selective retrievals. Third, complex record structures may waste computer disk and memory space. Some data base programs reserve disk and memory space for empty fields. If the monitoring program calls for collection of some data on a weekly basis and other data only on a quarterly basis, a complex record structure will require that space be reserved for empty fields in most records, since each record must include all fields and most records will represent weekly data.

3.2.D.3 Indeterminate Data

Indeterminate data are data that can be categorized as greater than or less than some value but cannot be more

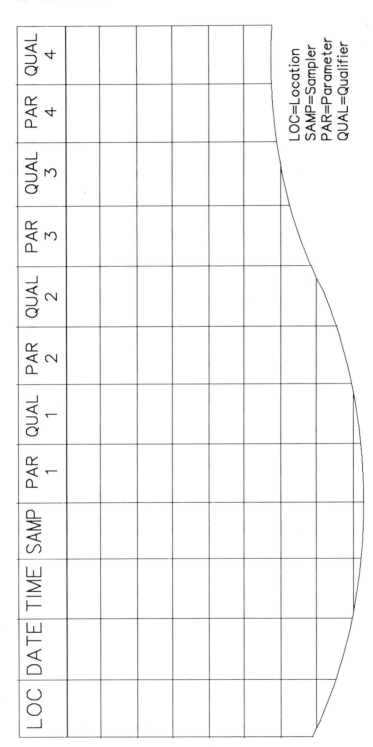

Figure 2 The complex record format provides easy computation using different parameters, by recording all parameters in a single record. Adding parameters requires modifying the structure of the data base.

LOC=Location
SAMP=Sampler
PAR=Parameter
QUAL=Qualifier

closely described. When chemical analyses fail to detect the target parameter, the results are reported as below the detection limit (BDL) of the analytical procedure. When insufficient dilutions are used in bacteriological analyses, the results are reported as being greater than a statistical estimator value. If microbial growth occludes a plate so that enumeration cannot be performed, the results may be recorded as too numerous to count (TNTC).

In the data base, indeterminate data results in the entry of some value in the value field and the entry of a flag in the qualifier field. In the case of a BDL result from a chemical test, the value field receives the detection limit of the analytical method and the qualifier field receives a flag such as a mathematical "less-than" inequality symbol that marks the BDL result. In the case of a bacteriological result greater than the table estimator value, the value field receives the estimator value and the qualifier field receives a flag such as a mathematical "greater-than" inequality symbol.

Indeterminate data must be flagged so that the results of mathematical computations are not compromised by using incorrect values. In the case of BDL chemical analysis values, there are several ways to address this issue. BDL values can be excluded from computations. Computations can be run using detection limit values, and the results of such computations can be expressed as less than the mathematical result since the data used to calculate the result are known to include values higher than the actual values. A simple probabilistic approach is to use half the detection limit in computations, assuming that for a large number of normally distributed BDL results about half the results would fall above that value and half below. If the data base is sufficiently large, there are statistical estimation or modeling techniques that can yield estimates of true values to be used in computations.

In the case of results above statistical estimator values, the results of computations using "greater-than" values can be expressed as being greater than the computed value, or computations can be performed using a subset of data which excludes the "greater-than" values. Where TNTC results are obtained, they must be excluded from computations.

3.3 CONSULTANTS

Computer system design consultants can be very helpful in designing the structure of the data base, selecting software, and selecting hardware to fit your goals. The trick is to make sure that the consultant's solution really meets your goals.

Computer consultants frequently face a frustrating dilemma. When they ask for the data management goals of the organization, the response is, "You are the experts—what should we do?" This is a question the consultant cannot answer. He may be an expert in computer systems, but you are the expert in your business, and running an efficient computer system is not your real business. You and your organization must go through the painful process of setting goals for your environmental data collection and management systems. Consultants can facilitate the goal setting process by conducting structured meetings, coordinating discussion groups, conducting systematic interviews, and organizing the inputs from all these processes.

Consultants may fall prey to the fallacy of recommending one of a few stock solutions for every problem. The commonalities among data management problems, the ease and satisfaction of implementing familiar applications, or the frustration of dealing with an organization that refuses to establish its own goals can make this occur without the consultant realizing it. Review the reports of the consultant to make sure that a wide spectrum of options was investigated, and that detailed, site-specific reasons were provided for the rejection and selection of options.

4

Software

4.1 GENERAL DATA BASE SOFTWARE

There are a number of general data base software products available commercially. These products allow users to create and manage data bases through user-defined field descriptions and through the use of query languages or menu-driven query systems. These products are available for both mainframe and personal computers. Several are produced in versions that operate on both mainframe and personal computer systems.

General data base software prompts users to create data bases by specifying field names, field types, field lengths, and other types of descriptive information. Field type refers to the type of data to be contained in the field, such as numeric data, text, or dates. Field types and definitions are specific to each software product. In most cases it is possible to create fields that are filled by computation involving data in other fields. In response to user input, the software creates fields with standard characteristics. The software also logs the field characteristics as a data base description, which users can retrieve for reference.

Many general data base software programs make use of add-on modules that supplement basic data management functions. These include report writers, spreadsheets, graphics, and form design modules. Report writers provide extra capabilities for report generation such as report titles, pagination, mathematical computation capabilities, and control over line and column formats. Spreadsheets provide additional mathematical functions and number manipulating capabilities. Graphics modules produce graphical representations of numeric data.

Form design modules provide the capability to produce user-designed data entry screens and query screens. For some products, these screens become a major part of data management. Different screens displaying different combinations of data can be designed to customize data retrievals for users and to limit data access for other users. Input screens may be the tools that implement the computation of fields whose contents are values calculated from other fields. Data input screens can provide a measure of quality control for the data base, for example by requiring entries in certain critical fields while making it possible to bypass other fields, or by screening data input to check that values fall within specified ranges.

4.1.A Advantages of General Data Base Software

General data base software packages possess several noteworthy advantages. These are summarized in Table 1.

4.1.A.1 Standardization

General data base software packages establish a set of commands for describing data bases and for manipulating data that are well documented in user manuals and do not change over time. This makes the system stable, makes it easier to modify the data base, and makes it easier to train users.

General data base software packages use uniform data storage formats. The designation of field characteristics (length, data type, etc.) causes the data base to treat each

Table 1   General Data Base Software

Advantages	Limitations
• Standardization	• Limited graphics capabilities
• Flexibility	• Difficult to program iterative operations
• Sophisticated data manipulation tools	
• Testing and debugging	• Limited mathematical and statistical functions
• Documentation	
• Product support	
• Software warranted, and maintenance available by agreement	

entry in a given field identically, regardless of the actual length of the entry. While this is not always the most efficient data storage format possible, it offers the advantage that the display of retrieved data is always consistent. This is a significant advantage over nonstandard data storage formats which often occur in customized data management systems. Programmers designing in-house data management systems are likely to use the data storage format that appears most efficient for the existing hardware configuration and application, such as a data string with elements separated by commas, rather than a more uniform format that reserves the same number of bits for each data element regardless of its actual length. When new data elements are added to a data base for which a nonuniform data storage format was used, and particularly when report formats must be altered, it becomes necessary to devise a method to insert null values for new data elements into the old data strings so they fit the new report format. This process can be difficult, especially if the original programmer is no longer available.

4.1.A.2 Flexibility

General data base software is highly flexible. Users design the data base themselves, and the design can easily be tested by using small data sets to identify desirable modifications.

General data base software packages provide relatively easy and safe procedures to modify the structure of fully loaded data bases, should it become necessary to do so.

4.1.A.3 Tools

General data base software products provide a variety of built-in tools for sorting, selecting, creating data subsets, and performing calculations with numeric data elements. General data base software products usually have the capability to import data files in standard formats, such as American Standard Code for Information Interchange (ASCII) and Data Interchange Format (DIF), and to export data in standard formats for use by companion software products. This ability to import and export data in standard file formats makes general data base software programs very portable, in the sense that the data contained in the data base can be easily transmitted in electronic format to other locations, other computer systems, and other organizations without the need for time-consuming and error-causing manual data entry.

4.1.A.4 Testing and Debugging

Complex software applications unavoidably contain internal processing errors and instances where modules that work properly individually fail to interface properly. An advantage offered by established general data base software products is that they have been subjected to extensive testing and debugging, both prior to commercial release and through the mechanism of customers finding the flaws in the system through intensive daily use. This offers an excellent prospect that an established commercial product will already have had most of its problems solved, and good approaches toward optimizing many applications that might fit your needs have already been developed.

4.1.A.5 Documentation

Thorough documentation is essential to the maintenance of any software application. General data base software products are extensively documented through user manuals, training manuals, programmer guides, system management manuals, etc. In addition, for products of even modest popularity, there is a wide range of third-party user manuals available. All these forms of documentation serve to assist the user in finding efficient ways to implement data base applications. They help to assure the long-term utility of the data base by providing a means of maintaining within the organization knowledge of how the data base software works.

General data base software also offers the advantage that the software is self-documenting. When a new data base is created, the software creates a log of the field designations and the characteristics assigned to each field. This makes it possible for future generations of users to identify the structure of the data base quickly and accurately.

4.1.A.6 Support

The corporations that market general data base software offer a wide range of support services. Various levels of training for users, system managers, and applications designers are offered. Often training can be provided at the customer facility using the customer's hardware, so that users are trained in their daily work environment. Telephone hot lines provide immediate assistance to users and system managers. Software products are warranted. Maintenance contracts provide for replacement of lost or damaged software and for upgrades to newer software versions as they become available. Disaster recovery services provide assistance in recovering data and in getting hardware and software back on line following fires or other natural disasters. Applications development assistance may be provided, where corporate specialists assist users in designing and implementing data base applications.

4.1.B Limitations of General Data Base Software

General data base software packages have several limitations that should be considered.

4.1.B.1 Mathematical and Statistical Functions

Most commercially available general data base software was developed with the business user in mind. The objective was to help large corporations manage huge volumes of data encompassing customer lists, sales, costs, overhead, inventory, personnel data, tax data, etc. The emphasis was on keeping track of data and on the ability to retrieve relevant data rapidly for any given situation. High order mathematical and statistical functions were not of interest. As a result, general data base software products do not provide the capability to perform calculations involving exponentiation or trigonometric functions. The built-in statistical functions are limited to simple descriptive statistics and to business-related functions. Additionally, different technical users have different needs, and it would become prohibitively expensive to satisfy all possible needs in addition to the basic data management functions for which the software was designed.

4.1.B.2 Graphics

Business graphics are highly sophisticated, utilizing line, pie, bar, and shaded area graphs, and even three-dimensional graphics. General data base software products provide only basic graphical functions such as simple pie, bar, and line charts in their basic packages. Again, it would be prohibitively expensive to provide the full range of graphics options available through computer technology, in addition to the basic data management functions.

4.1.B.3 *Programming Nonstandard Applications*

General data base software provides a simple means of accomplishing a number of universal tasks associated with data management. There are, however, certain tasks that require programming languages. Examples include iterative calculations, and unique data selection processes that the data base was not designed to support. Most products make it possible to save a series of data base commands in a file for data retrieval and formatting, and to execute commands from files. However, general data base software programs do not provide true programming capability equivalent to programming languages such as FORTRAN or BASIC.

4.2 SPECIALIZED ENVIRONMENTAL DATA BASE SOFTWARE

Several data base management programs on the market were designed for the management of environmental data. These are programs that were originally custom designed for a large organization, and later were marketed by that organization or by the software firm which developed the program. The advantages and limitations of specialized environmental data base software are summarized in Table 2.

Specialized environmental data bases may have more powerful built-in mathematical and statistical functions than general data base programs, because the specialized environmental data base programs were written with scientific applications in mind. Graphics capabilities are as limited as those of general data base software products. Iterative processes are not well supported. Specialized environmental data base programs tend to be industry-specific. A program developed for managing air emission data for an electric power utility may work well for other electric power utilities, adequately for other types of air emission monitoring programs, and poorly for water quality data. Customization of specialized environmental data base programs is frequently

Table 2   Specialized Environmental Data Base Software

Advantages	Limitations
• Powerful mathematical and statistical functions	• Customization difficult, requiring programming code changes
• Industry specificity can be advantageous if applied in the industry for which it was first developed, or in a closely allied industry	• Difficult to program iterative operations
	• Limited graphics functions
	• Limited testing and debugging
• Software warranted, and maintenance usually available by agreement	• Limited documentation
	• Difficult to obtain product support
	• Industry specificity can be disadvantageous if applied in a significantly different industry from that for which the software was originally designed

difficult. Customization requires changes directly in the program code, which is beyond the capability of most organizations unless there are professional programmers on staff.

Sale agreements for specialized environmental data base programs normally provide for training, and include some degree of consultation and program customization guaranteed under the software warranty. Since the industry-specific market for specialized environmental data base software is smaller than the market for general data base software, testing and debugging is not as thorough. Although documentation is provided with specialized environmental data base software, it is not as fully developed as is typically the case with general data base software. Further customization may be available through software maintenance agreements or simply on a time-and-materials basis. However, the process of familiarizing a programmer from the software provider with the special needs of your operation is time consuming. It may prove difficult to secure customizing services once purchase is complete and the software firm is in pursuit of other sales.

Table 3   Customized In-House Software

Advantages	Limitations
• Complete customization to present applications • Inclusion of desired mathematical and statistical functions	• Requires full-time programmer • Development time-consuming and expensive because of need to design and test system logic • Nonstandard protocols for data storage and processing • Limited data manipulation tools • Limited or no graphics functions • Limited or no testing and debugging • Poor documentation • Inflexible and difficult to modify • No warranty or availability of third party product support or maintenance

4.3 CUSTOMIZED IN-HOUSE SOFTWARE

Data management systems can be developed in-house using high-level computer languages. This technique provides the ultimate degree of customization and the opportunity to include desired mathematical and statistical functions, but it is not without drawbacks. The advantages and limitations of customized in-house software are summarized in Table 3.

In-house development of a data management system is an enormous undertaking. Having a full-time programmer on staff becomes a must, and the process of establishing an environmental data base becomes far more time consuming due to the requirements of logic design and testing. As a result, this approach is likely to be more expensive than purchasing commercially available software. It is seldom possible to provide graphics capabilities for systems developed in-house.

Developing data management software in-house is an exercise in reinventing the wheel. The task has already been done by both general data base management software and by specialized environmental data base software. In addition, commercial products have been debugged through extensive testing and through use by other customers. In-house products are tested and debugged using in-house personnel and data. Commercial products are warranted, use standardized procedures, and they are extensively documented. Software developed in-house is not warranted, and outside assistance with applications, software problems, and disaster recovery is not available.

The standardization and documentation offered by commercial software packages are of great value when the need arises to modify the environmental data base. With custom-written software, a programmer must make changes directly in the source code to effect any change whatsoever in the data base. Such systems are inflexible, and any change in application support requirements makes code changes necessary. This adventure becomes especially interesting when the programmer making the change is a different programmer than the one who designed the data management software. No matter how good the documentation, the new programmer still must understand the logic of the design and must ferret out all the interconnected modules and functions affected by the changes. Another difficulty is that programmers designing specific applications are likely to use the most efficient data storage format, such as a data string with elements separated by commas, rather than a more uniform format that reserves the same number of bits for each data element regardless of its actual length. When new data elements are added, and particularly when report formats must be altered, it becomes necessary to devise a method to insert null values for new data elements into the old data strings so they fit the new report format. Although writing customized data management software sometimes appears attractive, there are potential pitfalls.

Table 4   Types of Companion Software

- Spreadsheets
- Statistics package
- Graphics
- Word processors
- Desktop publishers
- Animation software

4.4 COMPANION SOFTWARE

The fact that general data base software programs generally provide only basic mathematical, statistical, and graphics capabilities was discussed in Section 4.1.B. This situation results in part from the fact that general data base software programs were designed for business applications. Another contributing factor is that such a broad range of potential capabilities exists that attaching even a significant portion of the available options to a single data base program would make the cost of the program prohibitive. Companion software bridges the gaps between high-powered data management systems that store and retrieve data, a variety of specialized data analysis needs, and the production of sophisticated reports. The major types of companion software are listed in Table 4.

4.4.A Spreadsheets

Like data bases, electronic spreadsheets may be thought of as ledger pages composed of rows and columns. Spreadsheets are programs designed to facilitate mathematical computation. Data are arrayed in the spreadsheet in a tabular format. The data can be displayed on a monitor, and the user can place data visually, as he would on paper. In this respect spreadsheets are very user friendly because of their "naturalness." The user constructs the mathematical formulas needed to accomplish computations and is able to use the results of computations in succeeding computations.

Spreadsheets provide a complete range of mathematical capabilities including exponentiation. Thus the most sophisticated mathematical and statistical calculations can be performed using spreadsheets. Spreadsheets incorporate a number of standard mathematical functions including trigonometric functions, logarithmic functions, and exponentiation functions. They include basic statistical functions that calculate the arithmetic mean, standard deviation, and maximum and minimum values for a set of numbers. Spreadsheets usually offer basic graphics capabilities as well.

Spreadsheets may be used as companion software to general data base management programs by exporting files containing data sets from the data base software to the spreadsheet for analysis. This enables the user to utilize a much wider array of numeric analyses than the general data base software provides. Both general data base software and spreadsheets can import and export ASCII files.

It is also possible to use spreadsheets as data entry modules for general data base software. The advantage is that a spreadsheet may enable the user to develop a highly sophisticated error checking system to screen data entry. In addition to ensuring that raw data fall within specified ranges, raw data may be compared numerically against quality control charts, checked for statistical distribution, or reformatted by preestablished spreadsheet formulas. Spreadsheets can be used for direct data acquisition from electronic sensors or laboratory instruments, reducing the incidence of transcription error. Raw data files created in spreadsheets can be reviewed for errors by multiple methods and individuals. When a data set is approved for entry, the spreadsheet can generate a data file that the data base software imports.

4.4.B Statistics Packages

Different scientific disciplines use different sets of statistical analyses to such a degree that it is difficult to recognize that all the techniques arise from a common science. Statistical software packages are specialized for specific fields of application such as biology, chemistry, medicine, or economics. Each package incorporates a set of formulas specific to the target discipline. In addition, statistical packages provide modules for manual data entry as well as for data entry via files. Like spreadsheets, statistical packages act as companion software by importing data sets from data base software as files and performing more sophisticated statistical analyses on the data than the data base software could provide.

A difference between spreadsheets and statistical analysis software is that statistical software packages incorporate specialized statistical formulas that a user can access and apply to data sets without having to construct the formulas. This provides ease of use and reduces the chance that a complex formula could contain an error. The advantage of the spreadsheet, on the other hand, is that the user is not limited to the statistical functions incorporated in the software package. The spreadsheet user can create any formula desired, at the expense of the user having to build the formula, and at the risk of the user making an error.

4.4.C Graphics

Graphics software provides several different types of functions such as creating graphical representations of numeric data sets, utilizing clip-art files for illustration, enabling the user to create personal graphical illustrations, and importing and editing scanned images. Graphics tools can be used to excellent effect in reports generated from environmental data bases to display data graphically, to illustrate trends and the relationships between parameters, and to highlight conclusions and important information.

Programs that create graphical representations of numeric data sets either allow direct keyboard entry of data or import data sets from files in standard formats. In many cases, they provide modules for working directly with other popular types of programs such as spreadsheet files and word processor files. These graphics programs generate a wide variety of graph types such as pie charts, bar charts, line graphs, and three-dimensional graphs. Options for different colors, shading patterns, and line types to distinguish and contrast different data sets displayed on the same chart are provided. A selection of typefaces and sizes for alphanumeric characters are offered to enhance the readability and professional appearance of the chart. Drivers for numerous types of printers and plotters are available.

Paint programs offer users the capability to create electronic drawings for use as illustrations. Paint programs for personal computers allow users to generate geometric shapes such as circles, ellipses, and triangles, as well as line segments, to create illustrations. These can be filled with colors or shading patterns, and multiple typefaces and sizes of alphanumeric characters are provided. Users can change the size and orientation and move portions of drawings, and image editing is provided. The ability to use clip-art for purposes of illustration is another feature. Clip-art files contain digitized images that can be incorporated into a report or brochure with tabular data or text.

Many paint programs can incorporate scanned images. With this feature and a scanning device, printed illustrations can be converted to digitized files. Then they can be edited, resized, and combined with data or text to add punch to a publication. The requirements and capabilities of scanner-supporting programs vary widely, but some offer very sophisticated capabilities.

4.4.D Word Processors

Environmental data collection must be followed by data analysis and interpretation. This process converts data into useful information. The next step is to communicate the information to decision makers, so that the activities of the organization can be guided on the basis of rational decisions. Written reports are the most frequent means used for communication, and word processors are the most common tool for producing reports.

Today's word processors offer far more than the basic abilities to change text electronically, to search for particular words, to replace phrases with other phrases, and to move blocks of text. The more popular word processors now offer on-line spelling checkers, dictionaries, and thesauri. They offer multiple typefaces and sizes for alphanumeric characters, and they are able to utilize an even wider range of soft fonts, providing virtually unlimited combinations of character printing capabilities to enhance documents. Modern word processors are able to import files from data bases and spreadsheets, which can be used to create tables in documents. They are also able to import image files or scanned images from graphics and paint programs, incorporating graphs and images into documents. They provide multiple-column formatting for professional-looking documents.

4.4.E Desktop Publishers

Desktop publishers go beyond the graphics capabilities of word processors and provide the ability to produce documents of the highest professional quality, previously available only through professional typesetting and commercial artist services. Desktop publishers often function as companion software to word processors and graphics programs. Word processors specialize in handling text, and graphics programs specialize in producing high-quality graphics. Desktop publishers specialize in combining text and graphics, providing tools for formatting text, for streaming text around images, and for creating a limitless variety of typefaces and sizes for lettering. Desktop publishers can import files from numerous other programs including spreadsheets, word processors, and graphics programs.

4.4.F Animation Software

Animation software enables a personal computer to perform like a slide projector, recalling a series of image files displaying text, graphs, or figures. Animation software usu-

Table 5   Benefits of Companion Software

- Ease of use
- Sophisticated, varied functions in specialized areas
- Inexpensive (PC versions)
- Can act as front-end modules to protect data accuracy
- Enhanced visual quality of data base output

ally makes use of a memory-resident program to capture screen images, generated by other programs, into bit-mapped files. These files record the color of each pixel, making it possible to reproduce the screen image exactly. The screen images can be cropped and edited as desired. Animation software provides different types of transitions (cuts, fades, and wipes) between images. The time of each image on the screen, and the duration of each transition, can be specified. An animated presentation is assembled by specifying a sequence of image files, the transitions between image files, and the timing of image display and transition speed.

Animated presentations can be highly effective in several formats. They can be used in lieu of slide presentations for briefing groups small enough to gather around a computer monitor. Often they can be produced more quickly and at lower cost than a slide presentation, since they eliminate the intermediate step of slide production. High-resolution projection equipment can make them suitable for use with large audiences as well. Unattended animated presentations can be used for public information displays, cycling a series of self-explanatory informational screens over and over.

4.4.G Advantages of Companion Software

The benefits to be derived from companion software are summarized in Table 5. Companion software is specialized by function. This makes it possible for companion software to offer a very high level of sophistication in a particular application at a reasonable cost. For example, a graphics program made to run on a personal computer could offer an extremely wide range of options for graphical presentation of data including different types of stacked and clustered vertical bar charts, horizontal bar charts, line charts with the option to shade the area between the data line and the horizontal axis, pie charts, and line/bar charts. Graphs could be shaded in eight patterns in addition to specifying six colors for use by peripheral devices. It could provide thirteen typefaces and almost an infinite range of text sizes.

Companion software written for personal computers tends to be far more user friendly and intuitive in operation than mainframe software. Personal computer software is marketed to users throughout the business world who have no time for computer jargon and who demand the ability to produce highly sophisticated printed materials with a minimum of training. Such software makes extensive use of user prompts, icons, and on-line help to steer the user through the program options.

The cost of companion software, especially for personal computers, is a very important feature. Personal computer word processing and graphics programs such as those described in the preceding sections are available for about $500, as little as one tenth the cost of equivalent mainframe software.

5

Hardware

5.1 HARDWARE CONFIGURATIONS

The needs of the organization determine the optimal hardware configuration for the establishment of an environmental data base. Environmental data bases can be established on any of several different computer configurations, depending on what makes sense for the organization. Configurations include mainframes with terminals, mainframes with personal computer (PC) workstations, PC networks, and individual PCs. These are diagramed in Figure 1. Some of the most important features of each configuration are compared in Table 1.

The distinctions among computer classes (mainframes, minicomputers, and PCs) have blurred within the past 10 years. It may be difficult today for the single user to distinguish between a PC and a mainframe on the basis of speed, multi-tasking capability, or volume of disk storage. Some of these distinctions have become a matter of option. The minicomputer class has been replaced by "small mainframes," which offer the same system architecture and use the same operating system and software as their larger cousins at a fraction of the cost. The ability to expand processing capability by clustering small mainframes into a network that is

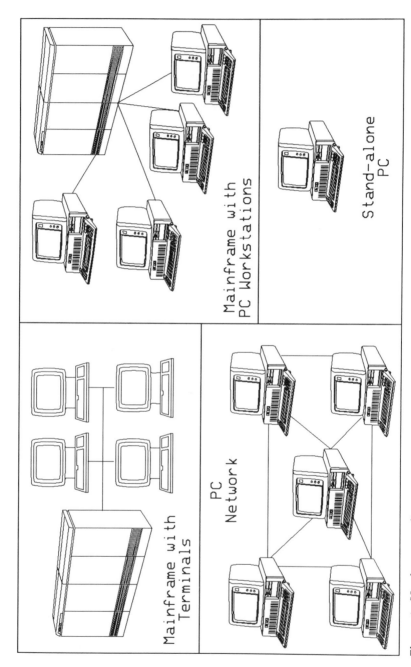

Figure 1 Hardware configurations.

Table 1 Comparison of Hardware Configurations

Mainframe with Terminals	Mainframe with PC Workstations	PC Network	Individual PC
• Users share DBMS, data, applications	• Users share DBMS, data, applications	• Users share DBMS, data, applications	• Offers automation advantages over manual data base management
• System maintenance, backup, and security are centralized	• System maintenance, backup, and security are centralized	• System maintenance, backup, and security are centralized	
• Multi-user access is facilitated	• Multiuser access is facilitated	• Multiuser access is facilitated	
• Large volume disk storage	• Large volume disk storage		
	• Processor-intensive applications can be decentralized to preserve mainframe speed		
	• PC-based functions are preserved during mainframe down time		
	• PC-based companion software is very sophisticated, user-friendly, relatively inexpensive		

invisible to users, and simultaneously to provide redundancy and backup in the event of failure of one machine, makes the mainframe option more affordable. Costs of mainframe computers have dropped dramatically, greatly reducing the economic barrier that once separated small organizations from the mainframe market. The availability of a broader range of capabilities in a broader range of machines creates great flexibility in computer hardware configurations.

5.1.A Mainframe with Terminals

Interactive access to mainframe computers can be provided by dumb terminals. The "dumb" designation indicates that the terminal has no independent processing capability of its own, unlike a PC. The terminal simply provides a link to the mainframe processor. All processing capability, all software, and all data files reside with the mainframe computer.

Establishing an environmental data base on a mainframe computer allows the DBMS and the data to reside in a central location where it can be accessed by all users. The mainframe-based system offers the potential for centralized system maintenance and easier routine backup of data files. Installation of a single copy of the DBMS is possible, reducing software maintenance requirements and providing standardization. The mainframe-based system helps to prevent the creation of nonidentical copies of the data base, which can occur in more distributed systems. Mainframe installation provides users the ability to share easily customized applications programs such as standardized reports and data retrievals. Mainframes offer larger data storage capability than PCs. Mainframes, through their physical architecture and operating systems, are designed to accommodate simultaneous access by a large number of users.

General data base software packages designed for mainframes offer record locking features, which prevent two users from accessing the same data record at the same time, although the time increment by which one user is denied access to the record may be so short as to be unnoticeable to the user. This feature prevents the case where two users, each with privileges to modify records, look at a record simultaneously and try to modify it. This could create errors in the data base, because transaction of one user will be processed first, so the second modification could act on data that the second user did not see. Record locking prevents the second user from gaining access to the record until the transaction of the first user is completed. When the second user is granted access to the record, all other users are locked out until the second transaction is completed. Record locking is an extremely important feature in data bases where multiple users have privileges to update records.

There are potential drawbacks to the mainframe-with-terminals configuration. The greatest is that if the mainframe or any significant component crashes, all users are left without computer access for the duration of the event. A second problem is that a large number of users may slow down the response time of the system significantly. Finally, software written for mainframes is several times more expensive than PC software packages that perform similar functions. Many pieces of PC software are equally powerful, more flexible, and far more user friendly.

Focusing computer applications on a single machine can be disadvantageous in the long run. This is particularly true when a single mainframe is the sole computing resource for the entire organization, providing services such as word processing and general purpose electronic spreadsheets that are accessed frequently. Applications such as word processing, which manipulate character strings extensively, slow down system operations tremendously.

5.1.B Mainframe with PC Workstations

Interactive access to mainframe computers can also be provided by PC workstations. The PC workstation is a stand-alone PC, connected to a mainframe computer by means of a communications device such as a serial port or a modem. The PC communicates with the mainframe using terminal emulation software. Terminal emulation software translates signals from the PC operating system into the format generated by specified types of terminals, so that the mainframe operating system is able to recognize and deal with them. The terminal emulation software also translates the signals from the mainframe so that they are understandable to the PC operating system. The PC has its own independent processing capability and its own data storage capability. The mainframe-with-PC option is more expensive than the mainframe-with-terminals option because PC workstations are more expensive than dumb terminals. However, the extra cost buys a great deal of added robustness for the system.

The mainframe-with-PCs configuration is a very powerful configuration that retains all the advantages of a mainframe-based environmental data base while solving the problems of the mainframe-with-terminals configuration. Commonly used applications such as word processing and general electronic spreadsheets can be moved off the mainframe to PCs. PC users have a wider selection of software packages, costing less than their mainframe counterparts and usually providing better utility. If the mainframe system crashes, PC users can still perform any PC-based operations.

Even users of the environmental data base that resides on the mainframe need not be shut down by a mainframe crash. Terminal emulation software makes it possible to download data files to the PC, where the data can be manipulated by a wide variety of PC-based companion software packages. Thus the environmental data base user can download data to his PC and perform subsequent manipulations and analyses independent of the mainframe.

5.1.C PC Networks (Local Area Networks)

Organizations that are relatively small, geographically centralized, and have limited computer requirements may find value in PC networks. PC networks are also referred to as local area networks, or LANs. The high cost of mainframe computers once made PC networks very attractive economically. However, falling costs have made small mainframes more competitive with PC networks.

PC networks emulate mainframe operations in several respects. One PC is dedicated as a file server for the system. Data files and applications software, including the DBMS and the environmental data base, reside on the file server. The file server is connected to the other PCs of the network via dedicated cables. Through communications software, the PCs access the file server and utilize its programs and data files as if they resided on the individual PCs. The capability exists to transfer data files between PCs and the file server, and each PC has its own processing capability. PC networks are geographically limited; they typically cover distances of no more than a mile and a quarter and often serve only a single building.

Networks preserve some of the advantages of a mainframe-based system. System management, maintenance, and routine backup can be centralized, and only one copy of application software packages need be purchased. Data and customized applications can be shared by users, and disk storage volume is not limited to that of the individual PCs. A potential advantage is that since PC networks are inherently PC-based, application software is PC software.

Networks can also fall prey to the disadvantages of the mainframe-with-terminals configuration, depending on how they are used. If many users rely on applications programs that reside on the file server, the system will lose speed. Any applications that reside only on the file server will be lost for the duration of a file server crash. These dangers can easily be overcome, of course, by distributing software and by downloading data files to individual PCs.

An additional management problem that may arise in PC networks is data base duplication. Assuming that a PC network serves a relatively small organization so that the size of the data base is inherently limited, it becomes possible to download the entire data base to one of the PCs of the network. The enhanced communications capabilities between devices on the network make it easy to add or delete data from downloaded files, using the DBMS located on the file server. The potential to create non-identical versions of the data base, which may not be readily distinguishable from one another, is greater than on a mainframe-based system.

5.1.D Individual PCs

Small environmental data bases can be maintained on individual PCs. The most obvious limitation is multiuser access. Unless the data base is cloned so that it can be run independently on different machines, access is limited to one user at a time. If the data base is cloned, multiple copies of the DBMS are required, and the danger of creating multiple versions of the data base is great. Situations can arise where it is very difficult to establish a "correct" data base, if different users are adding and deleting records simultaneously. Maintaining a data base on individual PCs means that there is no centralized file backup or system maintenance. These functions become the responsibility of individual users.

Maintenance of environmental data bases on individual PCs is suitable only in small organizations where the need for access is very limited. The two advantages of such a system are that it is the least expensive method of implementing a computerized environmental data base and that a computerized data base has many advantages over a manual data base.

5.2 DECISION FACTORS

In choosing a hardware configuration on which to implement an environmental data base, the real choice is between a mainframe-based system and a PC-based system. The advantages of mainframes over PCs are mass storage volume and the ability to accommodate larger numbers of multiple

Table 2   Hardware Configuration Decision Factors

- Applications
- Size of data base
- Number of users
- Geographic distribution of users
- Computer skills of users

users simultaneously without noticeable degradation in operating speed.

The factors that affect the decision on which computer hardware configuration to choose for implementing an environmental data base are summarized in Table 2.

5.2.A Applications Supported by the Data Base

Environmental data bases may be required to support a variety of applications including summary reports, regulatory reports, real-time operations control, research, and litigation support. Applications such as operations control or research, which demand simultaneous access by multiple users, may be good candidates for mainframe application.

5.2.B Size of the Data Base

The size of the data base and the storage capacity required for the DBMS determine the minimum disk storage requirements of the hardware configuration. The disk space required for data base storage can be estimated from the average record size and the number of records. Both the size of the existing data base, if any, and the rate of new record generation must be considered. Computer systems are not projected to have a long useful life because of the rate of technological change. A five-year period constitutes a long-range computer system plan.

PC hard disks are available in capacities exceeding 300 megabytes, and several external hard disks can be connected to a PC. Costs for PC hard disks increase exponentially as storage capacity rises above about 65 megabytes. A disadvantage of using multiple external hard disks on a PC is that disk access time lengthens. Another mass storage option for PC-based systems is removable hard disks (Bernoulli disks), which make it possible to use multiple high-capacity disks from a single disk drive. High disk storage capacity is a strength of mainframe computers. Mainframe architecture is designed to access multiple high-capacity disks rapidly. If the disk storage capacity requirements will exceed about 80 megabytes within the first five years, or if the rate of generating new records exceeds about 2000 records per year, it is at least worth investigating implementation on a mainframe.

5.2.C Number of Users

The number of users who need simultaneous access to the environmental data base affects the choice of hardware configuration significantly. If more than a single user at a time requires access to the data base, the option of a single PC-based system is eliminated, unless the organization is willing to run the risk of creating multiple versions of the data base. The number of simultaneous users that can be supported on a PC network without degrading operating speed depends on the processor and bus architecture of the file server, the capabilities of the file serving software, the topology of the network, and the capabilities of any communications controller devices used in the network.

The ability to give multiple users simultaneous access to an application, as well as giving users simultaneous access to different applications, is a strength of mainframe computers. If a number of users require simultaneous access either to the environmental data base or to other applications residing on the same system as the environmental data base, consideration should be given to implementation on a mainframe.

5.2.D Geographic Distribution of Users

The utility of single PC-based systems and PC network systems is limited to a small geographic area. If users in a PC network would be located much more than a mile from the file server, a network is unsuitable.

Users can be provided access to a central data base via modems, in either mainframe-based or PC-based systems. In either case, this requires the use of peripheral communications devices and interface software. Generally, mainframe computer architecture accommodates communications with remote users better than PC architecture. Communications protocols and software have been more extensively developed for mainframes than for PCs. However, if the environmental data base is small enough to be handled adequately by a PC, PC-based implementation is feasible.

5.2.E Computer Skills of Users

Establishing an environmental data base on a PC-based system probably requires the lowest degree of sophistication in terms of user computer skills. PCs have defined and refined the art of user-friendliness in a highly competitive marketplace. PC operating systems and applications software utilize extensive prompts, on-line help, and very readable manuals so that a lower level of prior knowledge is required on the part of the user. The familiarity of PCs and their ease of use can be an asset in getting environmental data base users started on the computerized system. A potential drawback is that the ease of using the computer system may encourage managers to expect users to learn the system by themselves. This is seldom an effective training method.

Mainframe operating systems and application software, being designed to take advantage of the expanded capabilities of mainframe architecture, tend to be more complex than their PC counterparts. This need not be a security hazard from the standpoint of accidental deletion or corruption of files, and it need not be a barrier to inexperienced users. Access to the system can be controlled in a manner that restricts the number of options each user can encounter. This can be done through a number of means including the use of menus that restrict user choices, batch files that automate a series of access commands, access and privilege restrictions associated with user names and passwords, and the use of directories and other mechanisms of creating logical disk partitions.

The mainframe-with-PC workstation configuration may require the highest degree of user skill. This configuration utilizes two different operating systems, one on the PC and one on the mainframe. Intermediate communications devices may be interposed between PC workstations and the mainframe. These devices, like automatic switching processors, control the assignment of users to a limited number of available communications ports on the mainframe. Terminal emulation software that enables communication between the PC workstation and the host mainframe must be learned. Many of these functions can be automated through the use of batch files and menus so that they become transparent to the user.

5.3 PERIPHERAL DEVICES

Computer systems used to implement environmental data bases should be capable of producing high-quality printed materials in order to maximize their effectiveness. These capabilities are provided through peripheral devices.

Laser printers produce high-resolution type, equal or superior to traditional letter-quality printers using daisy wheels or to typesetting. Laser printers simultaneously provide graphic printing capability, producing high-resolution graphs or pictorials. Laser printers provide the capability to include different typefaces and font sizes of lettering into documents to provide emphasis for key issues.

Plotters produce high-resolution graphs or pictorials using different types and colors of pens. Plotters are capable of producing colored graphics, and they are capable of producing transparencies for overhead projection and for overlays as well as paper graphics. Plotters provide a variety of typefaces and font sizes for inclusion in graphics, although plotters do not handle large text blocks as well as laser printers.

Film recorders convert digitized images directly to 35 mm color slides. This capability can be a very effective part of a public education program, in which the organization makes a series of presentations on a specific issue to different community, regulatory, or special interest groups. The ability to generate new slides quickly in order to tailor presentations to a specific audience can generate extraordinary dividends.

Scanners provide the capability to digitize printed graphics, so that they can be incorporated into documents or other computer-generated applications. Scanner-digitized maps are valuable accessories to environmental data bases. Scanners can also digitize pages of text into bit-mapped image files. These image files can be processed into ASCII text files by optical character recognition (OCR) software. This technique can be used to convert large printed documents, which were originally produced by some means other than computer, to files that can be revised or searched by a word processor.

6

Other Considerations

6.1 DEDICATED SYSTEM MANAGEMENT

The U. S. Army originally conceived the MAST (Military Assistance to Safety and Traffic) helicopter program as a simple matter of giving a physician a helicopter in place of an automobile. Upon receiving an emergency call, the doctor would dash to an aircraft, fly to the scene of the emergency, and administer emergency medical assistance. The system in its original form never got off the ground. Doctors proved to be surprisingly reluctant to add the hundreds of hours required to master helicopter piloting to their already long work hours and the effort required to stay current in their specialties. Fewer still displayed the ability to split their attention efficiently between controlling an unstable aircraft and treating life-threatening traumas. The Army discovered that both piloting and medical treatment are disciplines that require a tremendous degree of preparation and the full attention of the practitioner. Each job required separate groups of dedicated personnel. Environmental data base management is like that. Even the simplest single PC-based environmental data base requires some degree of system management in terms of making routine backup copies of the data base. When systems grow beyond the single user and single machine stage, and when managers want to use a computerized data base as a powerful tool but do not care to learn the details of how it works, computer system management becomes a full time job.

The value of the environmental data base demands dedicated system management. The organization has to be certain that the data base contains accurate and complete data. The data must supply a sound basis for management decisions and must provide a solid defense against unwarranted accusations and litigation. Sufficient resources must be dedicated to environmental data base management to assure that these basic goals are achieved. Two further decisions that must be made are whether dedicated system management should be provided in the form of a centralized data processing section or in the form of distributed data processing, and whether the responsibility for computer system management should be given to computer professionals or to business specialists trained in computer system management.

6.1.A Centralized vs Distributed Data Management

Often the organization that generates environmental data is a part of a larger organization. Examples are local manufacturing divisions of diversified national corporations, or operating divisions of municipal governments. Questions invariably arise as to whether the environmental data base should be maintained by the organization generating the data, or whether a centralized computer system operated by the parent organization should be used for data management. The benefits of centralized and decentralized data processing management are compared in Table 1.

Advantages of centralization include the potential for more effective computer system management, economies of scale, and standardization. Centralized data management sections employ computer specialists who are trained in the theory and practice of computer system management and who understand the operation of the hardware, software, and operating systems. They make the essential tasks of routine

Table 1   Centralized vs Decentralized Data Management

Advantages of Centralized Management	Advantages of Decentralized Management
• Economies of scale	• Focus on goals of end user organization
• Computer management by professionals	• No undue access restrictions to data or functions
• Centralized management, maintenance and security	• Timely response to support requests
• Standardized hardware and software make it easy for personnel to move within the organization and to perform routine tasks	• Willingness to experiment and change computer operations to provide better support to operations
	• Ease of communication
	• Specialized hardware and software is available at need to support mission-essential requirements efficiently

data backup, granting access to users, security, and other data management details a less onerous burden for the organization and can assure that they are accomplished in an effective and timely manner. Economies of scale are available to the extent that centralization reduces hardware and software duplication; multiple applications for various parts of the organization can be served on a single mainframe using single copies of software. Standardization of hardware and software makes it easier for personnel to move between sections of the organization without having to learn new computer operations.

Disadvantages of centralization, which argue in favor of decentralized data management, include focus on organizational goals, access to data, response time for data management needs, communication efficiency, and standardization. Most organizations, in either the public or private sectors, are in some business other than data management. Organizational goals and missions are directed toward producing products or providing services, and data management functions are ancillary to these goals. History shows that centralized data processing sections tend to develop technocratic empires within the larger organization. The goals of easy and efficient computer system operation begin to compete with the business goals of the parent organization and to interfere with operations. Data processing personnel sometime develop a proprietary attitude toward data and limit access to data and applications to a degree which impairs operations. Response to data processing needs is often slower when such needs must be referred to another section. A legitimate reason is that centralized data processing sections serving multiple other sections have data processing requests already in the queue which must be served in turn. A less legitimate reason is the resistance to changing an established system in order to preserve ease of operation, arguing that the request is either inappropriate or that it can be fulfilled by extra effort on the part of the requester. In large organizations, the geographic separation between data processing sections and operating sections can complicate the communication of data processing needs and reduce the sense of urgency for meeting those needs. Rigidly enforced standardization may well be counterproductive; there are numerous reasons why different sections of an organization may need specialized hardware and software to accomplish their jobs.

6.1.B Computer Specialist vs Business Specialist

The advantages of using computer specialists to manage a computer system include proper utilization of professionals and optimization of programming and computer system management. Employing computer specialists for system management allows professionals in other disciplines to concentrate on those disciplines, reducing the frustration of having to divide one's efforts among demanding requirements. Computer specialists are trained to optimize programming and the details of the computer management system. However, they often perform these functions without an intuitive

Table 2   Management by Computer Specialist vs Business Specialist

Advantages of Computer Specialist	Advantages of Business Specialist
• Proper utilization of specialists	• Proper priorities for computer section
• Optimized programming and computer system management	• More effective operational support
	• More timely response to support requests

understanding of the objectives of the organization. They can design applications to satisfy requests made by computer users, but may not be able to suggest modifications that would better utilize the capabilities of the computer system to serve organizational needs because they do not understand organizational operation. The benefits of having a computer system manager who is a computer specialist vs one who is a specialist in organization business are compared in Table 2.

It is easier to turn a trained professional into a computer operator than to train a computer specialist in another profession. An expert in business operations may face a large task in learning to manage a computer system, but he understands how the computer system is utilized as a tool to support operations. Computer system management and programming may not be optimally efficient but are likely to be more oriented toward support of the organization. With a business specialist converted to operate a computer system, there is apt to be more willingness to change applications to meet changing organizational needs, to serve needs more effectively, or simply for purposes of experimentation, than with a computer specialist who has optimized the computer system and likes the status quo.

6.1.C Personnel Backup and Continuity

With any essential element of business operations, provisions must be made to accommodate vacations and person-

Table 3   Elements of Data Backup and Verification

- Regular backup
- Off-site storage of backup data copies
- Regular data verification

---

nel turnover. Several people throughout the organization should understand the operation of the hardware and software systems, system management and data backup procedures, and the structure and contents of the environmental data base. This type of cross training may be more important than documentation. Hands-on experience eliminates the need to try to cope with difficulties using written procedures, and it enables much more rapid response. When computer system managers leave the organization, the continuity provided by cross training makes it possible for operations to continue unhindered during the process of personnel replacement and makes the process of indoctrinating new personnel much easier.

6.2 DATA BACKUP AND VERIFICATION

Computer systems fall prey to malfunctions from a number of sources ranging from hardware failure to operator errors to leaky roofs. Data entry errors compromise the validity and the usefulness of the environmental data base. Malfunctions can result in the loss of all or a portion of the data currently stored on mass storage devices. Regular and frequent data backup is important to minimize the impact of data loss and to speed the process of replacement. The essential elements of data backup and verification are summarized in Table 3.

6.2.A Regular Backup

A regular schedule of data backup should be established and rigorously maintained. The frequency and type of backup depends on the size and complexity of the data system and on the rate of generating new records in the data base.

In general there are two ways to perform backup. New files or expanded files can be copied to alternative storage media, or complete image backups of the entire contents of data disks can be made. For small systems, copying data files may be quicker. Complete image backups require more time, ranging from minutes for PC systems to hours for mainframe disks. Complete image backups have the advantage that executable software files are backed up along with the data. In the event of a system failure that physically damages a disk to the point where its contents cannot be restored, the complete image backup makes system recovery much faster and easier because replacement copies of software do not have to be obtained and installed.

Data backup can usually be automated to a large degree. PC operating systems contain backup commands that can be automated by incorporation into batch files. Mainframes that are powered up continuously but which are not monitored or accessed by users around the clock can be backed up daily using command files that execute automatically at hours when user access does not occur.

6.2.B Off-Site Storage of Backup Copies

An important purpose for backing up data is to preserve data from loss due to physical catastrophes such as fire and flood. This requires storage of backup data sets at a site remote from the computer system, where it is unlikely to be affected by a single event that might strike the compute center. At the very least, backup data sets should be stored in a building separate from the building housing the computer system.

It may be convenient to maintain two backup data sets, one in the computer center itself where it would be readily available in the event of a hardware failure or an operator error, and another at a remote site that is protected from physical catastrophes. A dual backup system requires more management to ensure that backup data sets are identical and current. It is not appropriate, for example, to store daily data backups in the computer center, and only store backup data sets to a remote storage site once per month. Such a system creates multiple backup data sets, and the most current backup set is the most vulnerable to accidental destruction. A physical catastrophe in the computer center just before the monthly backup to the remote storage site could cause the loss of an entire month's data.

6.2.C Data Verification

Data entry errors are inevitable, regardless of screening procedures. Incorrect data in the data base jeopardizes the validity of management decisions and legal defenses based on data analyses.

Data verification can be accomplished by general review of data to assure that entries are reasonable, or by detailed checking of entries against the original paper documentation. Detailed checking of all data records may not be feasible for a large environmental data base, but spot checking can be used to establish an acceptable confidence level.

6.3 DOCUMENTATION

Documentation is the primary means of recording essential facts about the computer system and the data base. Documentation provides continuity of data management operations when personnel changes occur and provides a basis for training. The essential elements of documentation are summarized in Table 4.

6.3.A Goals and Objectives

Documenting the goals and objectives of the environmental data base provides a record of the scope of the environ-

Table 4   Essential Elements of Documentation

- Goals and objectives
- Organizational commitments
- Data structure
- Software documentation
- Computer system operations

mental data collection effort and the uses intended for environmental data. This is important because it helps identify changes needed in the environmental data collection program in response to operational or regulatory changes. It may be an important means of justifying the maintenance or expansion of budgetary support for the environmental data collection program.

6.3.B Organizational Commitments

The support given to all programs varies over time. Environmental data base maintenance may be more likely than other programs to suffer a lack of enthusiastic support from management. Environmental data base maintenance is a long-term commitment that appears to be nonproductive and a drain on organizational resources when things are running smoothly.

Commitments made to environmental data base maintenance at the time the environmental program is initiated should be carefully documented to provide a record of the importance of the program to the organization. Documentation should discuss the consequences of a discontinuous data record, the managerial and legal applications of the environmental data base, and any expansions of the environmental data collection effort that were originally planned.

6.3.C Data Structure, Software, and System Operations

The structure of the environmental data base should be documented in detail. Documentation should include a brief description of alternative data structures considered and the reasons for adopting the selected alternative. This information is valuable both for applications development and for training. Documentation of data entry and retrieval procedures is contained in software user manuals. Customized applications such as data entry forms and routine reports should be documented to facilitate modifications as required and to facilitate training. Documentation of system operations is contained partly in user and technical reference manuals. Specific details of system management, including data backup and verification procedures, need to be documented separately to assure continuous system operation and to provide the rationale for standard operating procedures. Disaster recovery plans are an important part of operating system documentation.

6.4 TRAINING

Computer system training is a sore spot in many organizations. Users seldom feel they receive adequate training in the use of the computer system. Management sometimes feels that the expense of computer hardware and software is so great that they cannot afford expensive training for their personnel. Basic introductory training may be provided at the time the computer system is installed, but ongoing training frequently does not occur, and new personnel are often expected to learn computer system operations from existing employees through on-the-job training. In extreme cases, management may expect users to train themselves using hardware and software manuals and to accomplish their training in addition to their normal work loads.

Lack of a formal commitment to computer training is disadvantageous to the organization because it underutilizes the capabilities of the computer system and the environmental data base, and it frustrates employees. A commitment to a formal training program should be secured when the decision is made to implement an environmental data collection effort, and that commitment should be documented. A formal long-term plan setting forth different levels of training for different user groups, along with an implementation schedule, should be established. This plan should be supported by formal budget appropriations. Training should be an ongoing process. Effective training requires both formal instruction and the opportunity to implement the material presented through formal instruction. One-time training sessions are not adequate, because retention of instruction is never perfect, and full understanding comes only through experience. Training should be tiered, so that users are provided with more advanced instruction on the capabilities of the DBMS as they become more aware of potential applications for environmental data.

6.5 SECURITY

The two elements of data security are protecting the integrity of the data and controlling access to data. These functions must be properly balanced if the environmental data base is to be properly utilized.

Data integrity refers to maintaining correct entries in the data base and protecting against loss of records. The data base must be protected from sabotage—the deliberate introduction of erroneous data or deliberate deletion of records. Accidental deletion and corruption of data by authorized users must also be considered. This is accomplished by control of DBMS privileges, by password access procedures, and by control of physical access to computer hardware.

Both commercial DBMS products and computer operating systems have several levels of access control built in. Operating systems require validation of user names and passwords, at a minimum, to grant access to the computer system. Multiple layers of passwords, coupled with automatic abort routines if correct responses are not provided within specified time frames, provide effective barriers against computer system intrusion.

Commercial DBMS software packages provide the ability to restrict the level of access privileges granted to data base users. In addition to restricting access to some data sets completely, users can be granted privileges to examine data but not to add, delete, or change data. These features help to reduce the incidence of accidental corruption of the data base.

7

Personal Preferences

This book is intended for use by professionals responsible for environmental programs who are not computer professionals, but who are faced with the task of developing and implementing a computerized environmental data base. This chapter presents the author's personal preferences, which were formed through the experience of developing an organizational computer system and implementing an environmental data base. The author's preferences for environmental data base automation are summarized in Table 1. These elements might be regarded as an ideal system, but they would have to be verified for and tailored to each specific application.

7.1 DISTRIBUTED DATA PROCESSING

Bottom-level manufacturing or service divisions within larger organizations often have responsibility for conducting operations in a manner that assures compliance with discharge permits and protects the environment. Managers of these divisions have a vital interest in keeping the environmental data base up to date and in analyzing the data it contains because those data are the means by which compliance with permit limits and environmental law is assessed. Higher-level managers, and managers of support divisions such as centralized data processing services, have a less vital interest in maintaining the environmental data base. The organization that extracts the most useful information for use in supporting the decision making process is the organization that uses decentralized data processing to put bottom-level divisions in charge of the environmental data base.

7.1.A Ownership of System Management Personnel

Managers who are responsible for environmental compliance should control the computer system management personnel who maintain the environmental data base. Hiring of computer specialists should involve professionals from the centralized data processing organization in order that the computer skills of the applicants can be properly evaluated. But the computer specialists who operate the environmental data base system should be hired by the managers responsible for environmental compliance. The computer specialists who operate the environmental data base system should be housed in the operating facility so that they come to be familiar with the operation monitored by the environmental data base, and the data they manage take on meaning for them. The computer specialists who operate the environ-

---

Table 1   Recommendations

- Distributed data processing
    - ▶ Computer personnel report to end user organization
    - ▶ End user organization owns and manages the software and hardware
- Consultants used to aid selection of software and hardware configuration
- Hardware configuration: mainframe with PC workstations
- Software: general data base mainframe software with PC-based companion software
- System managed by an expert in the organization's business, supervising computer professionals

---

mental data base system should report to the manager of the operating facility so that the organizational lines of authority, responsibility, and loyalty are clear. This assures that when faced with a priority conflict between backing up the environmental data base or generating a mailing list for the company picnic, the environmental data backup comes first.

7.1.B Ownership of Software

Managers who are responsible for environmental compliance should maintain control of the DBMS software used to maintain the environmental data base. This allows the DBMS to be tailored to the needs of the organization responsible for environmental compliance, rather than forcing operating divisions to make do with DBMS configurations better suited for accounting operations than environmental data management.

This does not mean that the issue of compatibility between the environmental data base DBMS and other data management software used throughout the parent organization should be ignored. System-wide compatibility that allows easy data interchange among all computer nodes is important and should be preserved and enhanced to the maximum possible extent. However, older organizations may have established data automation systems that were developed in-house, many years ago, to support business and accounting operations. Environmental compliance needs may be relatively new to such organizations, and a natural first assumption may be that a computer system that has tracked millions of dollars and thousands of customers can handle a few sets of chemistry results with no trouble. The assumption is that the organization has to do the same types of manipulation and analysis with environmental data as with accounting data, and that assumption is disastrously false. The organization would be better served by letting its environmental data base needs drive the development of a modernized data management system than by trying to force environmental data management into an outdated financial system.

7.1.C Ownership of Hardware

Managers who are responsible for environmental compliance should own the hardware on which the environmental data base resides, as well as the equipment used to access and analyze environmental data. This is simply an expression of the principle that authority should reside with accountability; the person responsible for doing the job should be able to buy the tools needed. Managers responsible for environmental compliance should control expansion and upgrading of their environmental data base computer system as their operating requirements demand, and they should control access to their environmental data base computer system.

To the maximum practical extent, operating division managers should have budgetary control over their computer systems. Budgets for computer systems should not be reviewed separately from the rest of the operating division's budget on the assumption that computer systems are some special class of technology that requires special review. Computer systems that maintain environmental data bases are integral parts of the operating divisions responsible for environmental compliance, and they should be treated as such in the budget process. The high levels of liability associated with noncompliance with environmental laws demand such treatment.

7.2 USE OF CONSULTANTS

Environmental professionals charged with developing computerized environmental data bases definitely should use consultants. Environmental professionals are responsible for knowing what data are required, how those data are to be used, and who needs access to those data. Computer system consultants are responsible for knowing the full range of computer hardware and software products available to meet the needs described by the environmental professional. Using a consultant is a means of buying a higher position on the learning curve, and except in rare instances it is a cost-effective investment. Naturally, it is necessary to manage the consultant effectively to assure that the consultant is responsive to the needs of the organization and that the consultant has correctly understood the objectives. But it is often a more difficult task to ascertain and clarify the needs of the organization and to express them clearly to the consultant.

7.3 HARDWARE CONFIGURATION

The author's preference is a mainframe-with-PC configuration. In the author's system, a small mainframe computer (16 megabytes RAM, two removable hard disks with 450 megabytes capacity each, 5 direct access ports, 20 user ports allocated by an automated switching device) serves 22 user nodes in an organization of 137 personnel. Eight of these nodes serve users of the environmental data base. Most of the user nodes are PC workstations, although there are several dumb terminals in use. Each PC workstation has at least 640 kilobytes of RAM and at least 20 megabytes hard disk storage capacity. Peripheral devices available at different workstations include dot matrix printers, laser printers, plotters, and scanners. Modems are available to work stations through the switching device. The modems are used to download large data files from contractors who collect and analyze environmental data, and they are used to access several national computer networks used by the industry's professional organizations for information exchange through electronic bulletin boards.

This hardware configuration couples the power, sophistication, multiuser access, and large volume data storage advantages of the mainframe with the flexibility and independent processing power of PCs. The PC workstations offload many processing tasks from the mainframe. When the mainframe is inoperative, all day-to-day computer applications not related to the data bases residing on the mainframe are still available to the users. When specific work stations or peripheral devices are inoperative, all the other work stations, and the mainframe, remain in service. The impacts of device down time are very localized and minimal to the organization as a whole.

7.4 SOFTWARE

The author's preference is for general data base management software and extensive use of companion software. For the basic storage and retrieval of environmental data, the author's system uses a commercially available general DBMS configured for the mainframe. Data analysis, graphical presentation, and high-quality report preparation are performed using PC-based companion software. Data sets are generated on the mainframe through selective retrievals using the DBMS. Flat ASCII files are downloaded to the PC using terminal emulation software and manipulated as required using PC-based spreadsheets, graphics packages, and desktop publishing systems.

All word processing applications and spreadsheet applications reside on PCs. A single word processor is in use throughout the organization. A separate desktop publishing system is available at two workstations. Two spreadsheets are in use; the second was acquired specifically to interface with an automatic data acquisition system for laboratory instruments. Several different graphics packages, ranging from clip-art programs to computer-aided drafting and design programs, are in use throughout the organization. While the PC workstations have different hardware capabilities, they share a common operating system, so all the software and peripheral devices are available for use by any user simply by carrying a diskette to the appropriate workstation.

This configuration couples the power, sophistication, multiuser access, and large volume data storage advantages of the mainframe-based DBMS with the user-friendly, inexpensive, powerful features of PC-based companion software. This configuration makes a wide selection of PC-based software available to satisfy the different needs of individual users and provides drivers for a wide range of peripheral devices.

7.5 SYSTEM MANAGEMENT

The author's preference is for the computer system manager to be an expert in the organization's business while supervising a staff of computer hardware and software specialists. This is yet another means to assure that the computer system remains a tool dedicated to accomplishing the mission of the owning organization, rather than becoming an end in itself. In the author's organization, the computer system manager is a person who had more than 20 years experience in the field of wastewater treatment plant operation before the acquisition of computers to assist in data management. The computer system manager knows the business of the organization thoroughly. At least at this point in the organization's development, this assures that priority is given to those functions that support daily operations and regulatory requirements. The fact that the computer system manager is not a computer expert by training is insignificant; specific technical expertise can be purchased easily or hired as staff. The important point is that the system manager knows the business of the organization well enough to anticipate the ways in which computer support will be useful and to manage the computer system in such a way as to complement and enhance organizational activities.

Index